HERE COMES THE Bride!

KAREN MOORE

Bristol Park Books

First Bristol Park Edition published in 2018

Bristol Park Books
252 West 38th Street
New York, NY 10018

Bristol Park Books is a registered trademark
of Bristol Park Books, Inc.

Library of Congress Control Number: 2017957152

ISBN: 978-0-88486-676-3

E-Book ISBN: 978-0-88486-677-0

Text and cover design by Keira McGuinness
Cover art copyright ©2018 JuliyaM,Dreamer Light,/Shutterstock;
©Aleksandra Novakovic/Alamy

Printed in Malaysia

To

From

Date

Congratulations on finding the love of your life! May you live in sweet joy, wedded bliss and harmony always and in all ways. The two of you are sure to make many beautiful lifetime memories.

You have set out on a new path, and in it you will discover your great capacity for giving and receiving love. You'll learn, *you'll grow, and you'll cherish all that it means to share love for a lifetime.*

Enjoy every step of the journey.

THE SEARCH

The Search

I made a list of all the things
I wanted in a mate,
Hoping it would help me choose,
And even help me wait.

I wanted someone special
With a heart of purest gold,
Someone who would burst
with joy
Just having me to hold.
I wanted someone wise,
In all the ways that I was not,
And someone who would
talk to me
About the things I like a lot.

I wanted someone who
could laugh
And sparkle with the sun
And someone who on
meeting me
Thought life had just begun.

I searched with all my heart
For someone I could just adore,
And then we met, and I received
This list, and so much more!

My heart was
captured
By the light in
your eyes

There's Just Something About You

Something in your smile
Caught me by surprise,
And my heart was captured
By the light in your eyes...
There was just something special about you!

Something in our conversation,
Though I don't know all we said,
Simply touched my heart
And stayed inside my head...
Because there's something very special about you!

From the moment that we met,
A new song began to play,
A new melody was brought to life
That sings in my heart today...
Because there's something very special about you!

I thought about
our first date,
Long before
we even met

On Our First Date

I thought about our first date,
Long before we even met,
Knowing it would be a day
I never would forget.

I pictured how I'd smile
And fill your ears with nervous chatter,
Though nothing I would say just then
Would prove to really matter.

But something would be different,
It would be destiny or fate,
For we would know from that day on
We'd had our last first date.

I sense your
joy in being
near me

Along Came Cupid

Cupid steadies her aim,
unleashes her arrow,
and pierces an unsuspecting heart
with love.

Your Smile Speaks to Me

Your smile speaks to me
And I am warmed by your eyes.
I feel the touch of your hand
And I am calmer and happier,
Connected to the world in ways,
I've never known before.
I sense your joy in being near me,
And I'm aware of the gifts you bring to my life.

The music stopped. So did I

The Dating Dance

He nodded. So did I.
We headed for the swarm of warm,
Heated movement on the dance floor.
He looked absently about,
Sometimes noting he had a partner,
sometimes not.
I casually observed; seeing nothing,
seeing everything.
One swift movement and our hands touched
as he whirled me around.
The music stopped. So did I.
One more song and we danced again,
Slower this time.
The movement continued, elbows, fingers, toes...
Swirling, whirling, side to side, note by note.
Our eyes met. He smiled. So did I.
The dance continued.

The heart is a dreamer

What the Heart Knows

The heart is a dreamer,
And wanders alone,
Seeking love's call
All on its own.

It knows there is something,
Not easily defined
That will bring it true joy
And sweet peace of mind.

For the heart knows for sure
That nothing means more
Than discovering a love
Like never before.

So for all of the dreamers
And those hoping for bliss,
May your hearts fill with love
From the very first kiss.

Just Me, Just You

Blushing

There's a blush for won't and a blush for shan't
And a blush for having done it;
There's a blush for thought and a blush for naught
And a blush for just begun it.

Just Me, Just You

There's something really wonderful,
About being me and you,
Laughing, talking, holding hands
Loving all we do.

We're growing closer by the day,
And we're connected heart to heart,
We may not know the future yet,
But we're off to a great start.

Time to Meet the Family

Your nerves were slightly wacky,
Your smile somewhat strained,
You practiced just what you would say
And felt a little drained.
You smiled very kindly,
As you met each one by name
And tried to hide your nervousness,
As they tried to do the same.

Once you got to talking,
Things were off to a great start
And before you even knew it
You shared stories from your heart.
How quickly then, time slipped away
And when it was all through,
They said as you all hugged good-bye,
"It was so nice to meet you!"

FINDING THE RIGHT WORDS

Finding the Right Words

He may have stumbled through the words,
Or said everything just right,
But the day he popped the question
Filled your heart with sweet delight.

It wasn't easy for him
To find just the words to say
That meant you'd make a promise
To share your life and love that day.
Yes, that question popping moment
Changed your world and made it spin
Into a new direction
Where a new life could begin.
For it's more than just the words,
It's more than just a ring,
For now you have lifetime love
Which means more than anything.

Marriage means saying "I do" with every sunrise.

Our love was
meant to last,
And you were
meant for me!

Join Me at the Altar

Come join me at the altar
And be my lifelong bride,
Be my sweet companion
And my confidante and guide.

I promise that I'll be your friend,
And listen with my heart
And I promise that I'll always strive
To you love more, and do my part.
If you'll stay close beside me
Through all life brings our way,
Then we can face the challenges
And joys that fill each day.

Yes, join me at the altar
And I pledge to help you see
That our love was meant to last,
And you were meant for me!

As You Move Beyond "I Do!"

The love you share is tender,
Its promise bold and true,
But the love you feel
Will become more real
With each day ahead of you.

Bravely step into the future,
For all along the way
The love you know will gently grow
Stronger day by day.

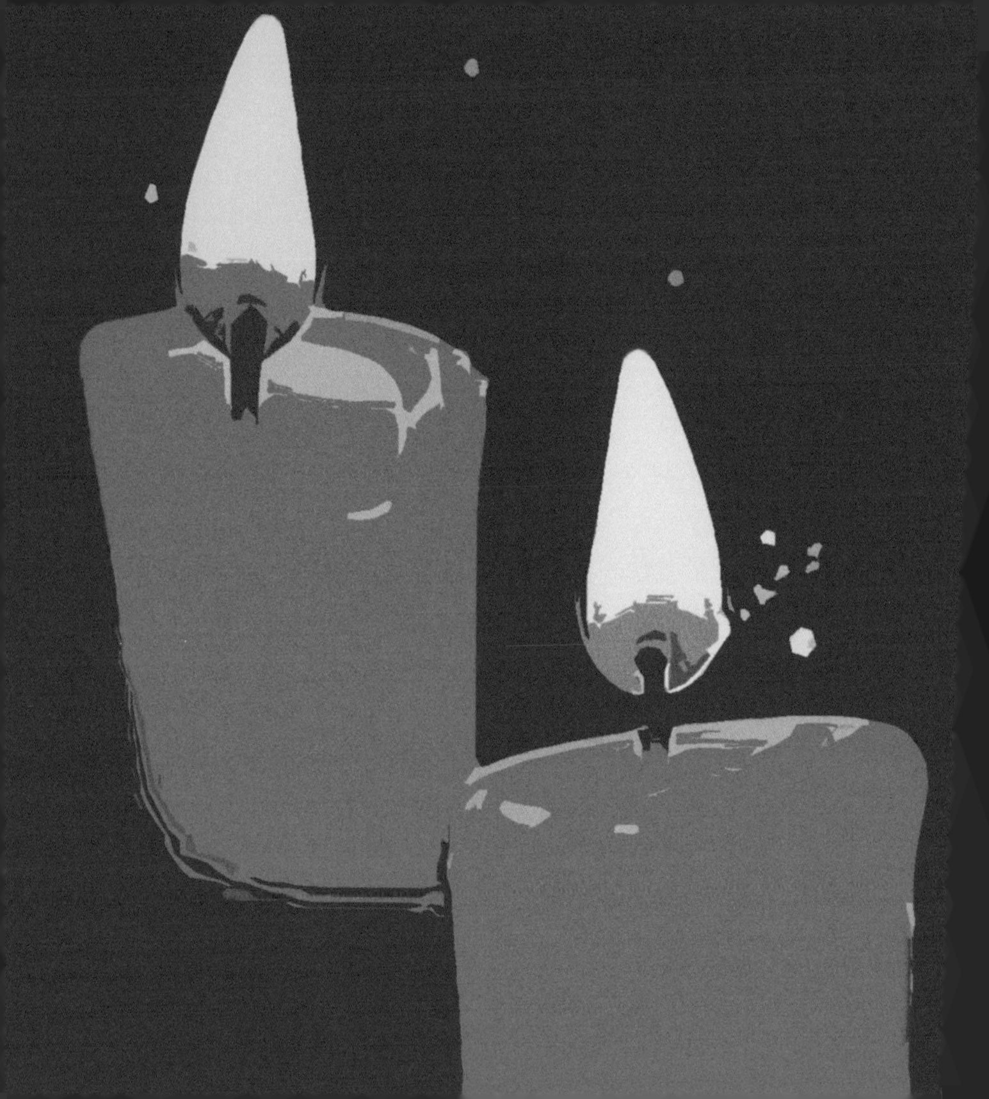

The Proposal

I'll remember that moment
For the rest of my life,
The one where you whispered
"Will you be my wife?"

You were tender and nervous,
A little unsure,
With a hope in your eyes
I never noticed before.

You took my hand
And held it so tight
As you waited for the answer
That would make things right.

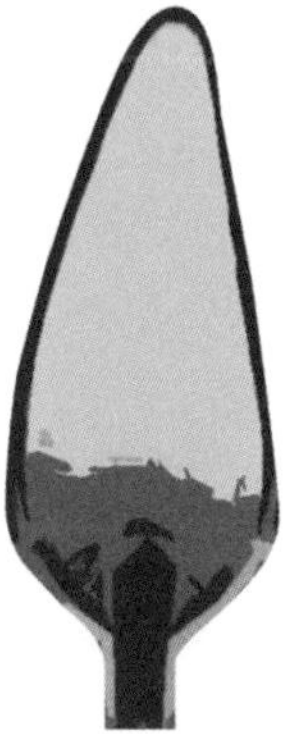

I was awestruck and marveled
At what you had done
And the promise you offered
To make our lives one.

You may have thought I waited,
To cause you to have to guess,
But I choked back tears of joy,
To answer with a "yes!"

I am yours
And my love can
hardly wait

My Questions Await Your Answer

Before I give my life to you,
Or offer you my hand,
Before I let the future in
Please help me understand...

Is there a heart that you hold still
That fills you with regret,
Some past love that will remain
That you never can forget?

Is there any part of all you plan
In the future we would share,
Where you don't see me stepping in
And always being there?

Is there a need that you might have
That I cannot fulfill?
Would you seek a former love
That you would hold to still?

Could you withdraw your love
one day
And take away my claim,
Saying this was a mistake
And I was all to blame?

Yes, now's the time to tell me
If you've cause to hesitate,
For if you don't, then I am yours
And my love can hardly wait.

My heart's as full as it can be

Shout it to the Mountaintops

I'd shout it to the mountain tops,
I'd raise my voice up high,
Letting all my happiness
Fill the earth and sky.

I'd tell it to the blue-green grass
And to the hills and trees,
I'd tell it to the flowers
As they dance with honeybees.

I'd tell it to the neighbors
And to the kids across the street,
And I'd tell it to my friends
And anyone that I might meet.
Yes, I'd tell everyone who'd listen,
My heart's as full as it can be,
Because someone "popped the question"
And wants to marry me!

The Wedding Plans

Should we marry in the summer,
Or the winter or the spring?
Should we plan a big reception
Or a family gathering?

Should we pick a favorite song
Or write each word to say,
Send a formal invitation
Or just announce the wedding day?

Should we be elegant or casual,
Have an awesome six-piece band,
Wear a gown and a tuxedo,
Should we kneel or sit or stand?

Should we fill the church
with people
Or just a special few,
Or should we plan to wed at home
With just a friend or two?

Yes, there's so much to consider,
So much to plan with great delight,
Because you chose your
lifetime love
And the future's warm and bright.

Just
Elope?

More Plans

We're making wedding plans
And everything is great,
We've found perfect invitations
And we've set the wedding date.

We've figured out the guest list,
And the grand reception hall,
And we'll have vases full of flowers
With vibrant colors of the fall.

We're excited with each step we take,
And filled with joy and hope,
But somehow all this planning,
Makes us want to just elope!

How do
I love
thee?

How Do I Love Thee? Let Me Count the Ways

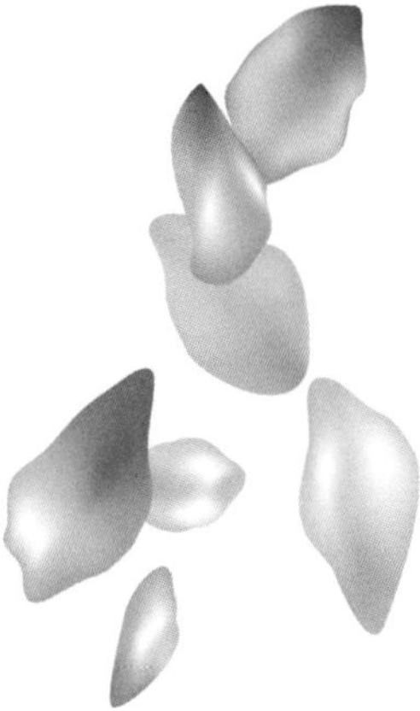

How do I love thee? Let me count the ways.
I love thee to the depth and breadth and height
My soul can reach, when feeling out of sight
For the ends of Being and ideal Grace.
I love thee to the level of every day's
Most quiet need; by sun and candle-light.
I love thee freely, as men strive for Right;
I love thee purely, as they turn from Praise.
I love thee with the passion put to use
In my old griefs, and with my childhood's faith.
I love thee with a love I seemed to lose
With my lost saints, --I love thee with the breath, Smiles, tears, of all my life!—and, if God choose, I shall but love thee better after death.

—Elizabeth Barrett Browning

IF YOU CREATE YOUR OWN VOWS

If You Create Your Own Vows...

I, (Groom), take you, (Bride),
to be my lifetime partner and wife.
I will share my life with yours,
look for ways to build our dreams together
and support you through times of difficulty.
I will always rejoice with you in times of happiness.

I promise to give you
my utmost respect, love and loyalty
through all the trials and triumphs
of our lives together.
I make this commitment to you with love.

I promise to keep it in faith, live it in hope,
and make it anew every day of our lives.

I choose you , ______________ because of who you
are and what you mean to me.
I commit to loving what I know of you, and trusting what
I do not yet know.

I promise to respect you as an individual, a partner,
and as my beloved, even more than my equal.

I promise to laugh with you when times are good,
and hold on to you when they are difficult for us.

I commit to you that I will always adore you, honor you and encourage you in every way that I can.

You are my best friend, and I promise from this day forward to love you always.

Groom: I promise to seek your advice and ask your help when I'm uncertain.
Bride: I promise to listen with love and share my own concerns.

Groom: I promise to tell you what's on my mind so you don't have to guess.
Bride: I promise to give you time to sort out your feelings.

Groom: I promise to surprise you now and then with flowers, or an unexpected date just to have fun.

Bride: I promise to always try to keep the sweet romance in our marriage.

Groom: I promise to keep you number one in my life, above my job, and my favorite sports team.

Bride: I promise to make it easy to be your number one in any way I can, and to root for your favorite team sometimes.

Groom: I promise to support you in whatever you choose to do.

Bride: I promise to support you in whatever you choose to do as well.

Groom: I promise to pay attention to details, the little things that mean a lot to you.

Bride: I promise to try to see the big picture and embrace your vision for us.

Groom: I promise to respect your mind and encourage your love of learning.

Bride: I promise to remind you of your talents and cheer for your successes.

Groom: I promise to pray for you each day.

Bride: I promise to pray for you as well.

Groom: I promise to tell you I love you and need you each day.

Bride: I promise to show you I care and that you matter always.

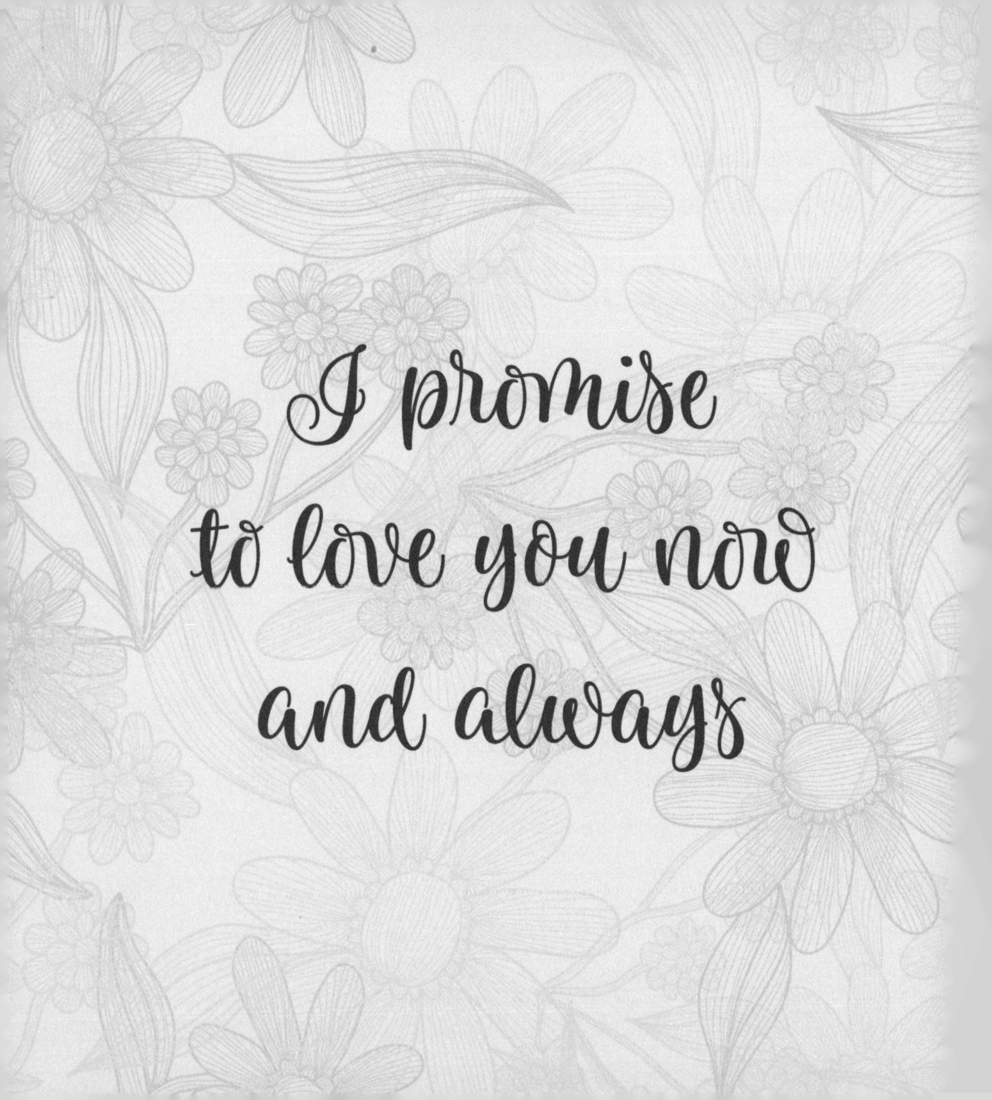
I promise
to love you now
and always

Groom: I promise to seek your opinions and trust your judgment.
Bride: I promise to ask your advice and consider your suggestions.

Groom: I promise to honor you, cherish you, and hold you in my heart forever.
Bride: I promise to hug you, kiss you, and cherish you always.

Groom: I promise to love you from this day forward.
Bride: I promise to love you now and always.

PLEDGES & TOASTS

If

If you can pledge to do your best
To help each other through
The challenges that marriage
brings
That test the "I love you." . . .
If you can give each other
The freedom to keep growing,
And talk about the things you
need
To help you each keep going ...
If you can face the little things
That come up, day by day,
And find you have the strength
of two
To chase them all away.

If you can look back where
you've been
And then look on ahead
And know that nothing matters
more
Than the joy of being wed...

Then you can have a marriage
That's a blessing and a blend
Of love and joy and laughter,
Heart to heart, and friend to
friend.

I promise that
I'll see you,
As the person
that you are

I Promise You

A promise is a pledge,
A sacred, lasting vow,
And so I promise you my love,
And my commitment now.
I promise that I'll hold you
When any doubts appear,
And I promise that I'll be there
In moments that bring fear.
I promise that I'll see you,
As the person that you are,

And encourage all your dreams
So that they can take you far.
I promise to apologize
When I do something wrong
And I promise that I'll
  do my best
To keep you safe and strong.
I promise to embrace our lives
To bring you joy and laughter,
Because I promise from this day
To love you forever after!

Here's to the
new husband,
and here's to the
new wife!

Simple Toasts

Here's to the new husband,
and here's to the new wife,
may they remain lovers,
for all of this life.

May all your hopes and dreams come
true, and may the memory of this day
become dearer with each passing year.

May the best of your yesterdays
be the worst of your tomorrows.

May the light of friendship guide
your paths together.

May the laughter of children grace
the halls of your home.

Bubbling Over!

May the joy of living for one another trip a smile from your lips, and a twinkle from your eye.

You've chosen to love for a lifetime, chosen to learn and grow together, and chosen to keep each other a priority.

May all that you've chosen be just the beginning of the joy you're meant to share.

WHEN THE WEDDING DAY IS OVER

When the Wedding Day Is Over

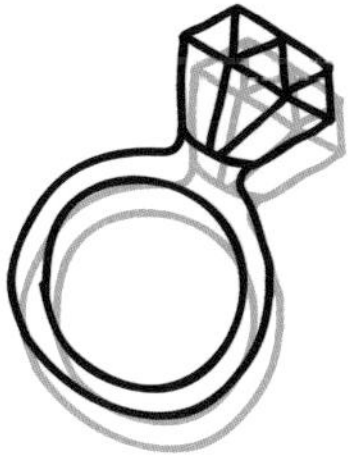

Oh, the wedding day is over,
The vows have all been said,
The songs have filled the chapel
And the Scriptures have
been read.

You're ready now to start again,
But this time not alone,
You're committed to each other
With a place to call your own.

You've stood before the altar
And promised all through life
To be each other's number one,
As a husband and a wife.

With rings upon your fingers
And smiles on your faces,
You're ready to embrace
the world
In all your favorite places.

May you long remember
all the gifts
Of your wedding day,
And may these forever
fill your heart
With love to guide your way.

Building Bridges

Let us build with art and soul, my dear,
A bridge of faith between your life and mine,
A bridge of tender love and very near
A bridge of understanding strong and fine—
Till we have formed so many gentle ties
There never will be room for walls to rise.

The Honeymoon

The honeymoon was
   neatly planned,
Each detail strictly noted,
Everything was perfect,
At least as it was quoted.

Yet, no one said that it
   might rain,
Or flights would cause delay,
Or there'd be no reservation
At the place you hoped to stay.

But, nothing really
   mattered then,
Because everything was right,
For you were there sharing love
Morning, noon, and night.

Yes, plans can sometimes
   go awry
Or they may go perfectly,
But your honeymoon begins
   the life
Where all your dreams will be.

Marriage
means you value
Each other's mind
and heart

What Does Marriage Really Mean?

Marriage means that you create
The things that make love thrive,
You hold hands everywhere you go
To keep your love alive.

You work hard on the courtship
That never has to end
And walk beside each other,
Arm in arm, and friend to friend.

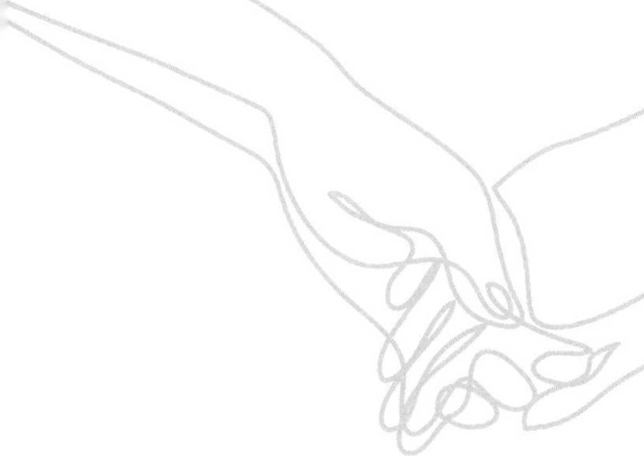

Marriage means you value
Each other's mind and heart
And that you feel a loss
Any time that you're apart.

It means you have a circle
Of new friends and family
That you both honor
and regard
With love and loyalty.

You'll
laugh a lot
And cry
a little too

Marriage means you understand
That when you know you're wrong,
You willingly apologize
So your love keeps growing strong.

Yes, marriage means you'll laugh a lot
And cry a little too,
But most of all and best of all
You're glad you said, "I do!"

MAKING A HOME

Hello!

Perhaps the sweetest words you'll say,
When you've been working hard all day
And found yourself forced yet to roam,
Are those sweet words, "So glad I'm home!"

Home Is the Place Where Love Resides

Home is the place where love resides
In each floorboard, wall and rafter,
Home is the place you hang your heart
And fill your days with laughter.

Home is the place where hope stops by
In the smiles of family and friends,
Yes, home is the place where love resides
And joy just never ends.

Setting Up Housekeeping

It's fun to pick new furnishings,
Or make hand-me-downs
 look cute,
But how we rearrange
 our things
May cause a slight dispute.

I like to have things orderly,
Clean and neat and put away,
You like to be more casual,
A little mess is quite okay.

Now we have to work it out,
Create a home to share
 our bliss,
So let's give each other lots
 of space
And seal it with a kiss.

Home Is Our Safe Haven

Home is where we sweep away
All the worries of the day
And with kind words and
 sweet delight
We guard each other through
 the night.

When I Need Your Love

I need your loving in the morning
Before my day begins,
Just holding me close
Starting with grins...it brings such perfect joy.

I need your loving in the noontime
When the world gets in the way,
When things feel more uncertain
And I struggle with the day...
because you make all the difference.

I need your loving in the evening
When the day is through
Because nothing in the world makes sense
Till I'm wrapped up in you...because you are my love!

My heart will always be at home with you

You may not be perfect,
but you're perfect for me.

The best choice I ever made was the choice to love you forever.

I keep falling in love with you...and I'm so grateful!

I loved you on our wedding day
And I love you even more today.

Marriage may require work,
but it's a job that has amazing benefits.

You're the best part of my life and you always will be.

I would marry you again in a heartbeat.

YOUR FIRST ANNIVERSARY

Your First Anniversary

The first anniversary
Is a precious milestone;
A measure of the things you've shared
And all the ways you've grown.

It's the perfect chance to reminisce,
Tell stories of the wedding,
And share again a special kiss
In joy at where you're heading.

Your first anniversary
Celebrates you two,
As a reminder of the life and love
That's still ahead of you.

Time is a weaver
And it threads
each thing you do

The Tapestry of Marriage

Marriage is a tapestry
Woven with such care,
That everything is intertwined
With loving things you share.

Time is a weaver
And it threads each thing you do
With ribbons of remembrance
And pearls of wisdom too.

Before you know it happened,
You're a couple on your own,
With a history of lace-filled dreams
And special ways you've grown.

Each of you weave separate dreams
Sweetly into one
Creating precious memories
Of all the things you've done.

Yes, it started with your wedding day
When you each held to a thread,
And started weaving stories
For all the days ahead.

May you both remember your wedding day
as the beginning of joy,
the moment when you made the best choice of your life.
May you each be a loving gift,
and an adoring presence,
for each other for the rest of your life.

May you both remember your wedding day as the beginning of joy

Illustration Credits

p1, images copyright © JuliyaM, Dreamer Light/Shutterstock; ©Aleksandra Novakovic/Alamy
p 3, image copyright © Svetlana Prikhnenko/Shutterstock
p 5, image copyright © JuliyaM/Shutterstock
pp 6-7, images copyright © mistletoe/Shutterstock
pp 8-9 images copyright © Moonybaka/Shutterstock
pp 10-11, images copyright © GoodStudio/Shutterstock
p 12, image copyright © Denis Sined/Shutterstock
p 13, image copyright © Ms VectorPlus/Shutterstock
p 14, image copyright © dikobraziy/Shutterstock
p 15, image copyright © Vladimir Curcic/Shutterstock
p 16, image copyright © ngagwang/Shutterstock
p 17, image copyright © nito/Shutterstock
pp 18-19, images copyright © Annakonst/Shutterstock
pp 20-21, images copyright © Margarita L/Shutterstock
pp 22-23, images copyright © everysunsun/Shutterstock
p 24, image copyright © RetroClipArt/Shutterstock
p 25, image copyright © Yubab/Shutterstock
pp 26-27 images copyright © anitaNP/Shutterstock
pp 28-29, images copyright © GulsevArtun/Shutterstock
p 30, image copyright © Chantall/Shutterstock
p 32, image copyright © LindsayC/Shutterstock
p 33, image copyright © Jemastock/Shutterstock
p 34-35, images copyright © Shorena Tedliashvili/Shutterstock
p 36, image copyright © chrupka/Shutterstock
p 37, image copyright © Olga Kononok/Shutterstock
pp 38-39, images copyright © Olga Kononok/Shutterstock
pp 40-41, images copyright © Yulia Sribna/Shutterstock
pp 41-43, images copyright © Brumarina/Shutterstock
pp 44,47, images copyright © AcantStudio/Shutterstock
p 46, image copyright © Chantall/Shutterstock
p 48, image copyright © Oaurea/Shutterstock
p 49, image copyright © Shavrina Vera/Shutterstock
pp 50-51, images copyright © YanaDesign/Shutterstock
p 52, image copyright © Irina Zharkova/Shutterstock
pp 53-55, 57, images copyright © zizi_mentos/Shutterstock
p 56, image copyright © Megan Tamaccio/Shutterstock
pp 58-59, images copyright © RATOCA/Shutterstock
pp 60-61, images copyright © Studio Barcelona/Shutterstock
p 62, image copyright © UliaMorenica/Shutterstock
p 63, image copyright © Yury Shchipakin/Shutterstock
pp 64-65, images copyright © Rvector/Shutterstock
p 65, image copyright © wan wei/Shutterstock
pp 66-67, images copyright © Yulia Sribna/Shutterstock
pp 68-69, images copyright © OJardin/Shutterstock
p 70-71,73,78, images copyright © Davdeka/Shutterstock
pp 74-75, images copyright © Eganova Antonina/Shutterstock
p 76, image copyright © Iuliia Pavlenko/Shutterstock
p 77, image copyright © Panda Vector/Shutterstock
p 79, image copyright © Baleika Tamara/Shutterstock
endpapers, image copyright © Tatiana Prikhnenko/Shutterstock